IMAGES
of America

FORT DAVIS

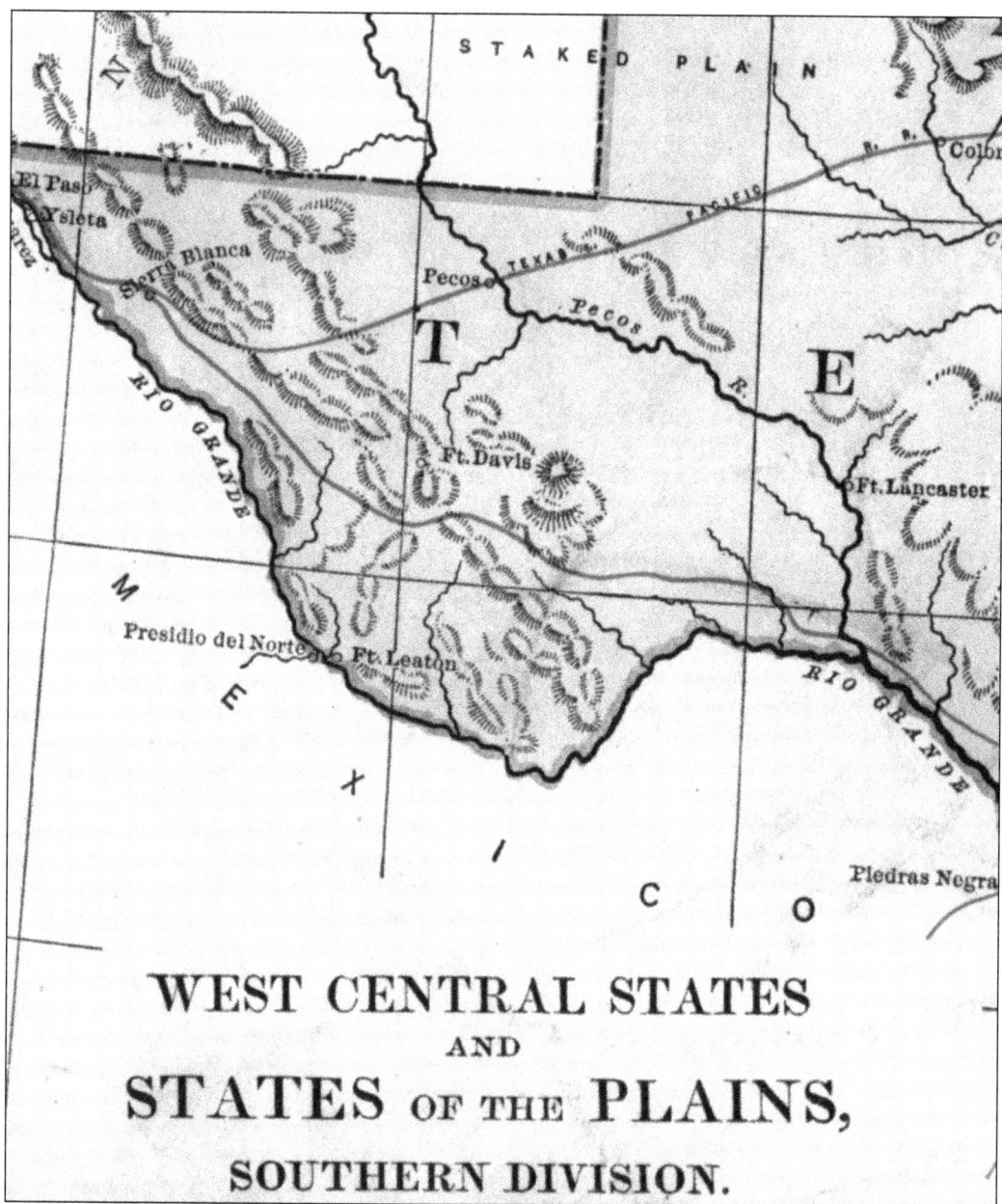

WEST CENTRAL STATES
AND
STATES OF THE PLAINS,
SOUTHERN DIVISION.

This map published by *Harper's Magazine* is a detail from "West Central States and States of the Plains, Southern Division." It locates Fort Davis and illustrates how sparsely settled and isolated West Texas was in 1875. (Courtesy of the Davis Map Collection, Museum of the Big Bend, Sul Ross State University.)

ON THE COVER: Looking south over the parade ground, Fort Davis is pictured in the late 1880s. (Courtesy of Fort Davis National Historic Site.)

IMAGES
of America

FORT DAVIS

Lawrence John Francell

ARCADIA
PUBLISHING

Published by Arcadia Publishing
Charleston, South Carolina

Library of Congress Control Number: 2011922886

For all general information, please contact Arcadia Publishing:
Telephone 843-853-2070
Fax 843-853-0044
E-mail sales@arcadiapublishing.com
For customer service and orders:
Toll-Free 1-888-313-2665

Visit us on the Internet at www.arcadiapublishing.com

*This book was only possible with the help and support of
my wife, Beth, and photo editor Jennifer Turner.*

With love to Emmy and Audrey.

CONTENTS

ACKNOWLEDGMENTS

As it turns out, relating history through photographs and limited captions is much the same as creating a museum exhibit where images are substituted for artifacts. In an exhibit, the artifact is key, and stories can only be told where there are objects available for interpretation—no artifact, no story. This project is much the same. There are numerous stories to tell, and many were left untold because there is no image. It was not for lack of effort, but gaps in the story are the sole responsibility of the author.

Many people made this book possible. Most important was Jennifer Turner, who did the photograph editing. The staff of Fort Davis National Historic Site, especially historian Mary Williams, was most generous. The Fort Davis Historical Society, especially Wid and Daisy McCutcheon, helped with unlimited access to the society's collection. Lucy Jacobson, coauthor of the official county history, was always there to answer questions, and her son Dave assisted greatly with photographs. Tom Barnes, Sandi Preston, and Jerry Wiant at McDonald Observatory helped immensely, as did Lisa Nugent at the Fort Davis Chamber of Commerce. When the next person undertakes a project of this nature, they will be seeking the collection of Max Kandler, who is on a mission to document everything that happens in contemporary Fort Davis. Thanks also to Martin Stringer, Julie McIvor, Betty Prude, Linda Hedges, Chuck Nowland, and others who so willingly helped.

INTRODUCTION

Texas has mountains—a fact that surprises some people. They rise up out of the plains in far West Texas as the ecologically unique "sky islands" of the Chihuahua Desert. This high desert ecosystem encompasses much of northern Mexico and stretches into New Mexico and West Texas. Among the largest of these ranges is the Davis Mountains, just north of the Big Bend of the Rio Grande. Nestled against these mountains is the village of Fort Davis.

For centuries, the mountains were the rich hunting grounds of Indians. The first European to pass through the region (in 1582–1583) was Antonio de Espejo. Soon, the Spanish had settlements along the Rio Grande all the way to northern New Mexico, but the more aggressive English and, later, Americans were pushing settlement from the east. Conflict was inevitable. Shortly after Mexico won independence from Spain (1821), that new nation had to contend with the boisterous Americans moving to the northern frontier province of Texas. The Texas Revolution and independence (1836) did not end the conflict with Mexico, which now centered on defining the precise border between the two countries.

The annexation of Texas by the United States (1845) led to war with Mexico, a continuation of this much longer conflict. The Mexican-American War (1846–1848) did not resolve all of the boundary issues, but it did result in the acquisition by the United States of the entire Southwest and California. Almost immediately after the peace treaty was signed, gold was discovered in California. This created two great national priorities: first, to define the border with Mexico and, second, to seek practical routes west to the gold fields.

For the initial Gold Rush forty-niners, the way west was across the prairie via the California Trail. Due to the heavy snows in the Sierra Nevada range, this route could only be used from spring to fall. Other options included passage around Cape Horn, which was difficult, dangerous, and time-consuming. One also could go by ship to the Isthmus of Panama, make the disease-ridden land passage from the Atlantic to the Pacific Ocean, and then continue on by another ship to San Francisco.

The first Americans to visit the Davis Mountains were soldier-surveyors seeking to establish the boundary with Mexico and to develop a suitable all-weather route to California. This road—known as the Lower Road to distinguish it from the Upper Road that ran from Fort Smith, Arkansas, through Guadalupe Pass to El Paso—began in San Antonio, where routes from various Texas port cities converged. From there it crossed Texas to El Paso, went across the New Mexico and Arizona territories to Yuma, and then progressed into California. Immediately, the Americans came into conflict with the diverse Indians who held prior claim to the land. In western Texas, this meant contact with the fierce Apaches, whom one contemporary observer described as the "Arabs of the American Desert."

The road had to be protected, and that task fell to the US Army. Most of the Army regiments were infantry—foot soldiers who were not well adapted to pursuing mounted and highly mobile Indians who felt their lands had been invaded. The solution was to build a chain of permanent installations across the Southwest that would allow the soldiers to patrol the road and, hopefully, keep any hostiles away from a vital US mail route and emigrants moving west by wagon trail to California. Where possible, these Army posts would be located at major water sources. This had a twofold advantage of providing the garrison with water and depriving the Indians of that same source.

Thus, in October 1854, Lt. Col. Washington Seawell, six companies of the 8th Regiment of the United States Infantry, and an extensive baggage train arrived to construct Fort Davis at the location known as Painted Comanche Camp on Limpia Creek. The actual post was located south of the creek in a sheltered canyon. Fort Davis was officially established on October 23, 1854, and named for Secretary of War Jefferson Davis.

With timber and stone plentiful, construction progressed rapidly, but the building methods and resulting structures were primitive. By 1856, there were six stone barracks with thatched roofs for the enlisted men, but most of the other structures were much less substantial. Lt. Zenas Bliss, who would serve at Fort Davis both before and after the Civil War, described his quarters as "about fifteen feet square and six feet high [from the] floor to the cross joints that would have supported the ceiling, if there had been any." His room was one of two into which the house was divided, and "the edges of the slabs were sewn [sic] off and the cracks where they joined were covered with battens. These had warped and the slabs shrunk so that the quarters did not lack ventilation."

From the beginning, the Lower Road was an important mail route. The first mail contract, from San Antonio to Santa Fe, New Mexico, was let to George Giddings, and in 1854, James Birch won the mail contract to San Diego. By 1859, the more famous Butterfield Overland Mail moved south from the Upper Road to continue transcontinental service. Both Birch and Butterfield operated until the Civil War.

The problems of communicating across the vast continent were so troublesome that creative solutions were sought. One of those was the possible use of camels. Under the direction of Secretary of War Jefferson Davis, 74 camels from the Middle East arrived in Texas in 1856. The camels passed three times through Fort Davis, the last time in 1860. For five days and 120 miles, they marched without water. The acting commander of the Department of Texas, Col. Robert E. Lee, reported that without their "endurance, docility, and sagacity, the reconnaissance would have failed." The coming Civil War ended the camel experiments.

In 1861, as the winds of war gathered in the East, the soldiers at Fort Davis and the other installations protecting the road concerned themselves with greater political issues. The election of Abraham Lincoln led to the dissolution of the country. In Texas, Gen. David Twiggs, Army commander and a sympathizer of the South, turned over Federal property to the new Confederate government and ordered his troops out of the state. Other than an unsuccessful invasion of New Mexico by forces under Gen. Henry H. Sibley, the Confederacy had little presence in West Texas, and Fort Davis fell into disrepair.

In 1867, the Army finally returned to the post on Limpia Creek, but this time it was the mounted troops of the 9th United States Cavalry under the command of Lt. Col. Wesley Merritt. He was determined to build a permanent installation with room for his mounted troops to maneuver. Merritt moved the post out to the front of the canyon, and over the years, it grew to over 60 buildings, most made of stone or adobe.

Once again, the primary mission was to protect the road. With mounted troops, the Army could engage the Indians on a more equal footing. During the most active years, from 1867 to 1881, the fort was manned by men from the four African American regiments—the 9th and 10th Cavalry and the 24th and 25th Infantry—known as the Buffalo Soldiers. Commanded by white officers, it was primarily these men who brought stability to the western frontier of Texas, opening the region for settlement.

The crucial period of conflict came between 1879 and 1880 during what was called the Victorio campaign. Not as famous a Geronimo, Victorio, a chief of the Warm Springs Apaches, found shelter in Mexico but often raided in Texas and New Mexico. It fell to the Buffalo Soldiers of the 10th Cavalry and their mild-mannered colonel, Benjamin Henry Grierson, to resolve the issue.

In a series of patrols, running firefights, and engagements at Quitman Canyon and Rattlesnake Springs, Victorio and his band were driven back into Mexico for the last time. He was eventually killed by the Mexican army.

One of the participants in the Victorio campaign was Lt. Henry Flipper, the first African American graduate of West Point. While there was mutual respect between Colonel Grierson and his junior officer, once Col. William Shafter took command of Fort Davis, circumstances changed. Flipper, who was both the quartermaster and commissary officer responsible for feeding and housing the garrison, handled a considerable amount of government funds. He came under suspicion of embezzlement. A subsequent court-martial found him innocent of these charges but guilty of conduct unbecoming an officer. Great controversy surrounded Flipper's court-martial, and in 1976, the Army changed Flipper's dismissal to an honorable discharge. He received a full pardon from Pres. Bill Clinton in 1999.

After the Victorio campaign, the high grasslands of the Davis Mountains attracted ranchers who began to move cattle into the region. As a consequence, the small town of Fort Davis that grew up to support the Army post developed into the commercial center of Jeff Davis County, which was organized in 1887. In 1883, the completion of the Southern Pacific Railroad created the second transcontinental line, but the tracks bypassed mountainous Fort Davis in favor of a more accessible route to the south through Marfa and Alpine. In June 1891, orders to abandon the post arrived at Fort Davis. Brig. Gen. David S. Stanley, the department commander, wrote, "Fort Davis had outlived its usefulness."

However, the community survived. Ranching was the primary economic force. Americans found leisure time and a new mobility with the advent of the automobile, and it was not long before the cool climate of the Davis Mountains attracted visitors. A large, comfortable hotel—the Limpia—was built in 1912 to accommodate those who the locals called "the summer swallows."

Beef prices held through World War I, and tourism across the nation increased through the 1920s. For a small village off the beaten path, Fort Davis prospered, but the Great Depression of the 1930s created havoc in the country, even in isolated places like the Davis Mountains. Cattle prices plummeted, and the nascent tourism business was curtailed. However, events that would have a far-reaching and future impact on the economy and development of Fort Davis were occurring.

As early as 1927, a bill instructing the Highway Department to develop the Davis Mountains State Park Highway through the heart of the mountains was introduced in the Texas Legislature. Actual work did not commence until 1932, and even then, the concept of the highway as a linear state park was soon set aside as New Deal agencies began to play a role in the country's recovery. In June 1933, Companies 879 and 881 of the Civilian Conservation Corps arrived and set up camp in Keesey Canyon, two miles north of Fort Davis. There they constructed the buildings and campsites for Davis Mountains State Park and the Indian Lodge, both of which are still major attractions. The Davis Mountains State Park Highway was never designated as such, but a 75-mile road through the mountains was eventually completed after World War II and is now designated the Scenic Loop, another major attraction.

In 1926, the University of Texas at Austin received a bequest from William J. McDonald of Paris, Texas, to establish an astronomical observatory. The university had no astronomy department, nor a location. The academic problem was solved by a partnership with the University of Chicago, which had an excellent department. Austin would pay for the telescope and find a location, and Chicago would supply the astronomers. The site chosen was on the G.S. Locke ranch, about 12 miles from Fort Davis. The land was donated by Violet Locke McIvor and named Mount Locke in honor of her grandfather. Additional acreage was donated by the estate of Edwin H. Fowlkes.

Construction on the dome for the initial 82-inch telescope began in 1933, and the McDonald Observatory was dedicated on May 5, 1939. Since then, the site has grown into one of the largest and best-known astronomical complexes in the world.

Unassociated with the McDonald Observatory complex and originally part of the Harvard University astronomy program is the Harvard Radio Astronomy Station. Because of a low level of electronic interference in 1956, Fort Davis was chosen as the site for a 28-foot-diameter radio antenna dedicated to solar observation. In 1963, an 85-foot-diameter radio antenna was added. In 1991, the station and antenna became a unit of the Very Long Baseline Array of the National Radio Astronomy Program.

On July 4, 1963, Fort Davis National Historic Site was created as part of the National Park Service. Today, the old fort stands as a reminder of the nation's frontier heritage and the conflicts with the original inhabitants here. The National Historic Site, McDonald Observatory complex, The Chihuahuan Desert Research Institute, Davis Mountains State Park, Indian Lodge, and the Scenic Loop through the heart of the mountains bring visitors to this unique place. At the same time, the old historical ranches still exist, and cows grazing along the highway fence lines are a common sight.

In 2008, Fort Davis was named one of the country's dozen "Distinctive Destinations" by the National Trust for Historic Preservation, and in 2009, the town was listed as the "Best Small Town in Texas." In 2010, Fort Davis was third in *True West* magazine's "Top 10 Western Towns." With its high desert climate and dark skies, Fort Davis is a hidden treasure unique to Texas.

One

GUARDING THE ROAD
1854–1861

In the period before photography became common and transportable, the first images of Fort Davis consist of a series of watercolors by Capt. Arthur T. Lee, 8th Infantry, who served there from 1854 to 1858. In *Fort Davis, Texas*, the post at the mouth of the canyon is to the far left, and Limpia Creek, an important water source, is to the right. (Courtesy of the Rochester Historical Society, New York.)

The first Europeans to explore the Southwest were the Spanish. These explorers, or conquistadores, and the priests that either accompanied them or soon followed were said to be seeking "God, Glory, and Gold." The Spanish approach to exploration and discovery is graphically illustrated in this work by the artist, Jose Cisneros. The first European to enter the Davis Mountains and camp along Limpia Creek near present Fort Davis was Antonio de Espejo. Espejo came to New Spain in 1571 as an officer of the Inquisition. After running afoul of the law and to escape punishment, he sought permission to lead an expedition north. From November 1582 until September 1583, he led his men across the Rio Grande at the present site of Presidio, Texas, traveled north to near Santa Fe, and followed the Pecos River south, diverging from that watercourse to enter the Davis Mountains. Following Limpia and Alamito Creeks, he returned to Presidio without incident. He discovered no riches. (Author's collection.)

As the guns fell silent at the end of the Mexican-American War, gold was discovered in California. Forty-niners rushed to California, making transportation and communication routes a national imperative. This map, created by Army topographical engineers under the command of Lt. Col. Joseph E. Johnston, while lacking in detail, delineated the first usable routes across Texas. (Author's collection.)

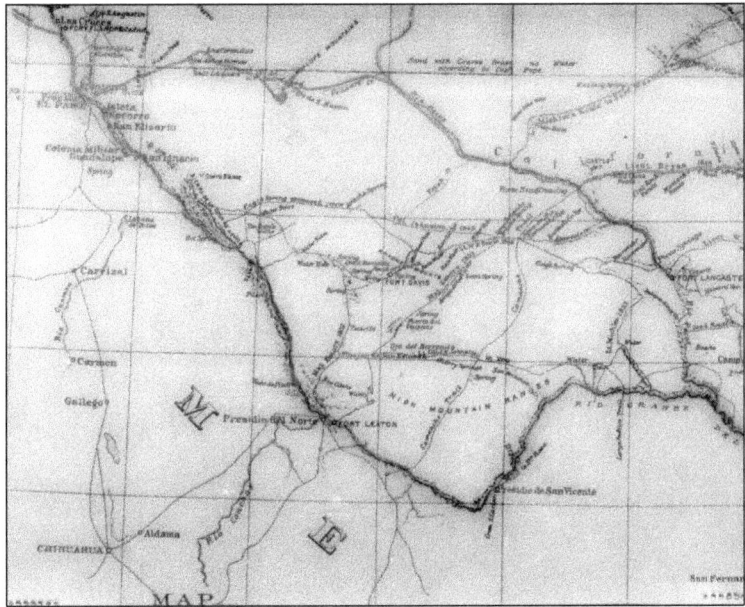

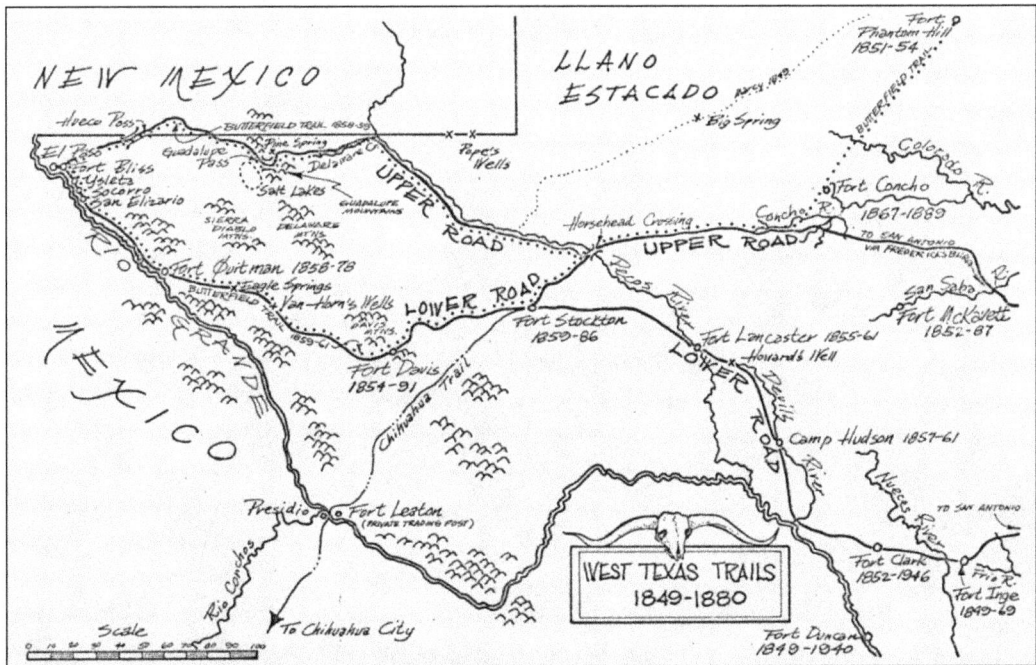

This contemporary map illustrates in greater detail the trails, mountain ranges, settlements, and forts of West Texas. The Upper Road passed through the Guadalupe Mountains of Texas, and the Lower Road, also known as the Military Road, passed through the Davis Mountains and Fort Davis. (Courtesy of Jerry Harlin.)

Across the great American West, most of the men responsible for marking boundaries, surveying rivers, and laying out roads were members of a unique military unit: the Army Corps of Topographical Engineers. Only the top graduates of West Point were assigned, and they crisscrossed the west from the end of the Mexican-American War until the Civil War. Wherever the Corps and Army conducted their surveys, encampments such as this could be found. (Author's collection.)

Entry into the Davis Mountains from the north is through Wild Rose Pass and along Limpia Creek. This illustration of the mountains was made by the men of the US Boundary Commission, who camped in the pass in the summer 1852. This location would later become a stage stop on the overland mail route through Fort Davis. (Author's collection.)

Of course, the country was not devoid of human habitation. To the immediate east were the Comanches, and the Davis Mountains were home to the fiercest Apaches the Americans would encounter in the Southwest. The difficulty was compounded in the pre–Civil War period when the majority of western posts like Fort Davis were manned by infantry rather than the more maneuverable cavalry. However, Congress, citing greater costs, was unwilling to increase the number of mounted regiments. Dr. J.D.B. Stillman, a physician from New York on a cross-country adventure, spent several months in West Texas, even serving as temporary post surgeon at Fort Lancaster located to the east of Fort Davis. He encountered Apaches more than once and described the situation as such: "what can they do without horses against these Arabs of the American desert? As well might dragoons be used as marines on the deck of a frigate." This image, one of the first of an Apache, is from Maj. William H. Emory's *Report On the United States and Mexican Boundary Survey*, 1856. (Author's collection.)

EMIGRANTS ATTACKED BY THE COMANCHES

The Indians fiercely defended their homeland. As more immigrants moved west, particularly to California along the southern route through the Davis Mountains, protection became imperative. The Army responded by creating a series of forts along the Lower Road from San Antonio to California. This engraving by Capt. Seth Eastman illustrates a classic confrontation between Indians and emigrants moving west. (Author's collection.)

Capt. Arthur Lee captures the essence of the relationship between the Indians and a nation moving west in his watercolor titled *Comanche Overlook*. (Courtesy of the Rochester Historical Society, New York.)

16

In 1854, the commander of the Department of Texas, Gen. Persifor Smith, personally inspected the western portion of his department to select the best site for a new post. Arriving at Painted Comanche Camp in early October, he located a new fort in a canyon just to the south of Limpia Creek. The site provided natural shelter, good water, wood, and grazing for livestock. (Courtesy of Fort Davis National Historic Site.)

On October 7, 1845, Lt. Col. Washington Seawell, six companies of the 8th Infantry, and two wagon trains carrying supplies, headquarters material, and the regimental band arrived on Limpia Creek to establish Fort Davis. A graduate of West Point in 1825, Seawell fought in the Seminole wars and would serve as commanding officer at Fort Davis for most of the period before the Civil War. (Courtesy of Fort Davis National Historic Site.)

Fort Davis was named for Secretary of War Jefferson Davis. Davis, later president of the Confederacy, worked to reform the Army, encouraged the experiment with camels as transportation in the Southwest, and directed the Pacific Railway Surveys, the first scientific and systematic survey of the American West. (Courtesy of Fort Davis National Historic Site.)

Protecting the road to California was the Army's primary mission. Construction of the post was secondary, so Fort Davis was a haphazard affair and built of the materials at hand, as illustrated in this watercolor by Capt. Arthur Lee. (Courtesy of the Rochester Historical Society, New York.)

The random layout of Fort Davis is best illustrated in this map drawn by the Army's inspector general, Joseph K.F. Mansfield, in 1856. (Courtesy of Fort Davis National Historic Site.)

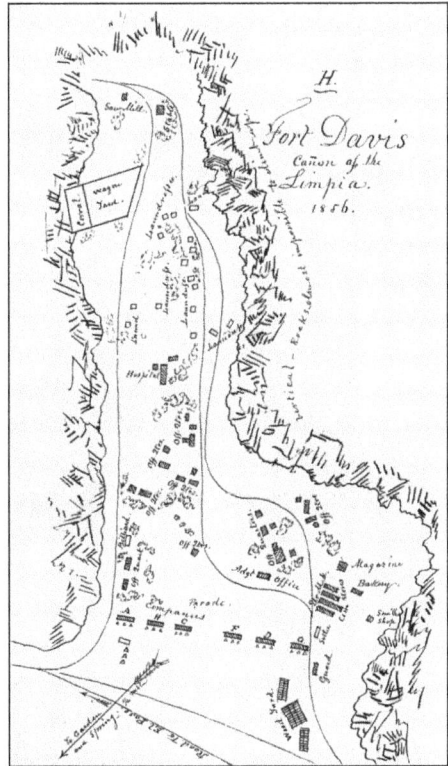

Zenas Bliss, a Civil War Medal of Honor winner who served at Fort Davis before and after the war, described the prewar fort as follows: "the post was the most beautiful situated of any I have ever seen. The quarters were very poor. . . . They were built by the labor of the enlisted men and no other persons were employed and the post probably did not cost the government $1000 except for the lumber." (Courtesy of Fort Davis National Historic Site.)

19

With the end of the Mexican-American War in 1848, the strength of the Army was reduced to 10,000 men assigned to protect hundreds of miles of coastline and the interior West that stretched from southwestern deserts to the Pacific Coast ranges. This lithograph by Henry Ogden illustrates the Army uniforms of the period: major general and staff and line officers. (Courtesy of Fort Davis National Historic Site.)

In this period before the Civil War, the US Army was fundamentally undermanned and underfunded. With a small and disorganized command structure, much depended upon the quality of the officers in the field. This Ogden lithograph illustrates the uniforms of staff, field, and line officers. (Courtesy of Fort Davis National Historic Site.)

The Army consisted of eight regiments of infantry and six of artillery used mostly for coastal defense. There were five mounted regiments: the 1st and 2nd Cavalries, the 1st and 2nd Dragoons, and the Regiment of Mounted Rifles. While mounted units were superior in the pursuit of hostile Indians, these five regiments were not enough to cover the West. Infantry had to suffice at most of the frontier forts. Here, Ogden illustrates the period uniforms of the cavalry and dragoons. (Courtesy of Fort Davis National Historic Site.)

Unable to respond quickly, the soldiers at Fort Davis had to content themselves with patrolling the road, enlisting for five years and earning $11 a month—if the paymaster arrived on time. The uniforms of the enlisted men are illustrated in this Ogden lithograph. (Courtesy of Fort Davis National Historic Site.)

Before the Civil War, thousands of settlers and gold seekers passed through Fort Davis on their way west, as illustrated in this watercolor of Wild Rose Pass by Capt. Arthur Lee. (Courtesy of the Rochester Historical Society, New York.)

The Lower Road was also an important mail route. The first contract was let in 1851 to Henry Skillman. By 1859, the famous Butterfield Overland Mail passed through Fort Davis. This watercolor by Capt. Arthur Lee captured the local overland stage station, which can only be described as primitive. (Courtesy of the Rochester Historical Society, New York.)

The mail and stagecoach passengers, unless under escort, were especially vulnerable to attack. In his travelogue, *Beyond the Mississippi* (published in 1867), Albert Richardson describes an attack on the mail where the Indians became so engrossed in the papers they captured that they were consequently surprised by an Army patrol. (Author's collection.)

INDIANS SURPRISED AND DEFEATED IN LIMPIA CANYON. Page 234.

In 1855, Secretary of War Jefferson Davis persuaded Congress to make an appropriation for funds to import and experiment with camels as transportation in the Southwest. On several occasions, the camels passed through Fort Davis, as illustrated in this watercolor, *Camels Crossing a Western River*, by Henry Sindell. (Courtesy of the Amon Carter Museum of Western Art, Fort Worth, Texas.)

23

When Texas seceded on March 4, 1861, Gen. David Twiggs, a southern sympathizer commanding the Department of Texas, ordered Federal troops out of Texas and turned over most of the property under his control to state authorities. (Courtesy of Fort Davis National Historic Site.)

In March 1861, as Federal troops left Texas for the conflict in the East, *Harper's Weekly* published an article that included this last illustration of Fort Davis in the prewar period. (Author's collection.)

Two

SETTLING THE FRONTIER
1867–1891

Once Federal troops abandoned Fort Davis, the post fell into disrepair. A few civilians remained in the community of La Limpia, which had developed to serve the garrison and the overland mail station. For a brief period, Confederate Company D Texas Mounted Rifles garrisoned the fort, and a New Mexico invasion force commanded by Brig. Gen. Henry H. Sibley passed through hoping for victory but returning in defeat. (Courtesy of Fort Davis National Historic Site.)

On June 29, 1867, two years after the end of the Civil War, Federal troops returned to the abandoned post on Limpia Creek. These soldiers were four troops of the 9th Regiment of Cavalry under the command of Lt. Col. Wesley Merritt. He was an 1860 graduate of West Point and a distinguished cavalry officer who went on to command US troops in the Philippines during the Spanish-American War. (Courtesy of Fort Davis National Historic Site.)

LT. COL. WESLEY MERRITT, 9th Cavalry, reactivated Fort Davis in 1867 and commanded the post until 1869.

The men of the 9th Cavalry who arrived with Merritt were members of one of the four African American regiments organized after the Civil War, the Buffalo Soldiers. For the next 18 years, units of these regiments would call Fort Davis home. There are few photographs of the Buffalo Soldiers, but there are great drawings created by Frederic Remington, such as this one, A *Campfire Sketch*. (Author's collection.)

Merritt moved the post to the mouth of the canyon and was determined to build a substantial fort large enough to muster the garrison, with a parade ground, officers' quarters on the west side, and enlisted barracks on the east side. (Courtesy of Fort Davis National Historic Site.)

In the initial flurry of construction, the first officers' quarters were constructed of stone. In this early photograph (1871), the first stone quarters have been completed, and the ruins of the original fort barracks are in the background. These were eventually torn down and the materials recycled for construction of the new post. (Courtesy of Fort Davis National Historic Site.)

One of the carpenters who found his way to Fort Davis was Edward Hartnett. Listed as a carpenter at a salary of $75 per month in 1867, Hartnett continued on at various jobs until he died at age 39 in October 1884, the longest-serving civilian at Fort Davis. His descendants still live in the community. (Courtesy of Fort Davis National Historic Site.)

Probably as a cost-saving measure, only 7 of the 11 officers' quarters were constructed of stone. The rest were built of adobe, but to make them all appear alike, these six homes were plastered with a tinted material that matched the stone color, and lines mimicking cut stone were etched into the plaster. Visitors today can see the vestiges of the original tinted plaster under the porches of several of these structures. (Courtesy of Fort Davis National Historic Site.)

No 2.

Across the parade ground on the east side, barracks for the enlisted men were constructed of adobe. Eventually, there would be four barracks fronting the parade and two others behind this line to the north and south that formed a quadrangle with privies and bathhouses. Each barrack consisted of two squad rooms, a mess hall, a kitchen, and storerooms. High ceilings with cupola ventilators and large porches made these comfortable quarters for the day. These images date from 1871 (above) and around 1875 (below). The original post guardhouse is seen in the foreground of the 1871 photograph. (Both, courtesy of Fort Davis National Historic Site.)

Construction at any frontier fort was ongoing. Repairs and new construction were a daily process and combined the labor of both civilians and soldiers. Life at a frontier garrison consisted primarily of duties at or near the post, not chasing Indians. In 1870, enlisted men earned $13 per month with an extra 24¢ a day tacked on for fatigue duty, the tasks required to keep the post operational. (Courtesy of Fort Davis National Historic Site.)

With so much activity in the area, a civilian community began to develop across from the military reservation, as seen here, looking over the quartermaster's corrals. By the early 1870s, there were almost 200 civilians working at the fort, supporting the stagecoach line, or supplying the fort in one manner or another. (Courtesy of Fort Davis National Historic Site.)

Like the enlisted men, the officers lived in relative comfort in homes well constructed for the period. Married officers most often had their wives and children present. They made the most of the accommodations at frontier forts and provided a civilizing influence. In letters and journals, Fort Davis is often listed as a good duty station. (Courtesy of Fort Davis National Historic Site.)

While the quarters may have been comfortable, there was a strict hierarchy relative to their selection. In a process known as ranking out, a senior officer could choose the quarters of anyone he outranked. The next officer would likewise choose, and the dominos would fall in succession of rank. (Courtesy of Fort Davis National Historic Site.)

Numerous activities were necessary to support a frontier garrison. Fort Davis had storehouses, a granary with many tons of corn and oats for the hundreds of horses and mules, stables for the cavalry, and corrals and work areas for the quartermaster, who was responsible for supplying the post. Designated spaces included a wagon yard, wagon repair facilities, and a blacksmith's shop, as well as shelter for wagons and mules. There was a commissary responsible for supplying the garrison with food, a bakery, barracks for the regimental band, a chapel, headquarters, and the necessary guardhouse. This photograph (1887) includes these areas and, in the foreground, the sutler's store. The sutler was a civilian with a contract to serve the garrison. (Courtesy of Fort Davis National Historic Site.)

While much of the life of the garrison centered on the parade ground, the most important building on post was likely the hospital. The Fort Davis Hospital is tucked away in a sheltered part of what is known as Hospital Canyon. Architecturally unique, it is one of the most significant public buildings of 19th-century Texas. (Courtesy of Fort Davis National Historic Site.)

The present hospital was constructed in 1875 to replace a temporary structure. Initially, this was a main building housing the post surgeon, hospital steward, dispensary, kitchen, and various storerooms. Attached was a north patient ward with 12 beds. In 1884, a 12-bed south ward was added. Today, one may visit the recently restored hospital. (Courtesy of Fort Davis National Historic Site.)

The post surgeon was a staff officer. As such, he also had responsibility for the quality of the water supply, living conditions, cooking and sanitary conditions, the bakery, and even the post garden. He was often called upon by the civilian community for medical care. As an officer, he lived on the line, observed the military schedule, served on details and court-martials, and produced a variety of reports. (Courtesy of Fort Davis National Historic Site.)

While the post surgeon was responsible for all aspects of health, medicine, and sanitation, it was the hospital steward who was the first point of contact for most soldiers who fell ill. A senior noncommissioned officer, the steward oversaw much of the day-to-day operation of the hospital. His home was to the south, or left, of the hospital. (Courtesy of Fort Davis National Historic Site.)

If the assumption is that wounds from conflicts with the Apaches were common, that was not the case. Battle wounds were rare—as rare as actual contact with hostile Indians. There were, in fact, more cases of accidents and violence within the garrison than wounds in battle. Many more men died of illness, especially respiratory and gastrointestinal diseases.

The Sign Language, seen here, is the work of Frederic Remington. (Author's collection.)

There were few battle wounds because most of a soldier's time was spent in the garrison, on duty at the sawmill, manning a sub-post that Fort Davis maintained, or on patrol, where encounters with the Indians were rare. One activity that occurred daily was a dress parade, usually retreat, at the end of the day. Here, the garrison is seen in full dress on the parade ground in 1889. (Courtesy of Fort Davis National Historic Site.)

Dress uniforms of the period, following a European model, were ornate and designed to develop an esprit de corps. The dress uniform was worn only on parade or special occasions and had trim and plumes that designated the various regiments: yellow for cavalry, red for artillery, and light blue or white (with a spike on the helmet) for infantry. This lithograph by Henry Ogden illustrates the uniforms of the period: officers and enlisted men in campaign dress. (Author's collection.)

Uniforms were made of wool, but it was the footwear that prompted the most complaints. Produced at the military prison at Fort Leavenworth, they were crudely made and uncomfortable. On campaign, the soldiers wore their oldest clothing, and regulations were more relaxed, but as stated in the song "Regular Army-O," "the USA never changes they say, but continually wears the blues." Here, Ogden illustrates the full dress uniform for officers and enlisted men. (Author's collection.)

The story about the pursuit of Apache leader Geronimo in Arizona is one of the better-known events from the Indian wars. In the lesser known but just as important pursuit of the Apache chief Victorio, the Buffalo Soldiers of Fort Davis proved their value in a campaign that began in New Mexico and stretched from 1879 into 1880. (Courtesy of Fort Davis National Historic Site.)

The Apaches consisted of several groups whose homelands ranged from Arizona through New Mexico and into far west Texas. As a people, they were seminomadic, excellent horsemen, and fierce fighters who often raided in small groups using hit-and-run tactics. Bringing them to bay was never easy. (Courtesy of Fort Davis National Historic Site.)

The first action of what became the Victorio campaign occurred in New Mexico when Victorio and his followers jumped the Mescalero Reservation and the 9th Cavalry, under the command of Col. Edward Hatch, took up pursuit that lasted into the spring of 1880. Before taking command in New Mexico, Hatch was commanding officer of Fort Davis in 1870. (Courtesy of Fort Davis National Historic Site.)

By May 1880, Victorio had escaped into Mexico. The commanding officer of the 10th Cavalry in Texas, Col. Benjamin Henry Grierson, was convinced that the next foray would be into Texas planned accordingly. Rather than wear down his men in long and unprofitable pursuit, he decided to station troops at known crossings on the Rio Grande, at mountain passes, and at water holes (as illustrated here in A Pool in the Desert by Frederic Remington). Accordingly, he moved his headquarters from Fort Concho to Fort Davis. (Author's collection.)

Benjamin Henry Grierson was born in Pittsburgh and raised in Ohio. At the outbreak of the Civil War, he volunteered, joining the Union cavalry, and had experience marching troops when, in May and June 1863, he led a 16-day raid from LaGrange, Tennessee, to Baton Rouge, Louisiana. Disrupting the defenses and communications and destroying supplies behind Vicksburg, the raid made Grierson a Union hero. (Courtesy of Fort Davis National Historic Site.)

COL. BENJAMIN H. GRIERSON, 10th Cavalry, played a significant role in the Victorio war of 1880 and commanded Fort Davis from 1882 to 1885.

Grierson's strategy paid off. In the two major engagements of the conflict—Quitman Canyon, July 30, 1880, and Rattlesnake Springs, August 5, 1880—Grierson was able to quickly concentrate his forces and drive his foe away from critical water sources. Here, a cavalry charge is illustrated by Frederic Remington. (Author's collection.)

In July, Victorio once again crossed into Texas. Grierson realized that the Apaches would need the water available at Tinaja de las Palmas, so he determined to fortify the water hole before the Apaches arrived. He set off to do so with Lt. William Beck, five troopers, and his son Robert, of whom he said, "[he] was out in search of adventure and suddenly found it." The Historic Site museum has a diorama depicting this battle. (Courtesy of Fort Davis National Historic Site.)

Robert Grierson, 19 years old and recently graduated from high school in the family hometown of Jacksonville, Illinois, arrived in West Texas in time to join his father in the Victorio campaign. Robert kept a journal of that summer's adventures, a most interesting and delightful document. Present at the Battle of Quitman Canyon, he wrote, "the rifles sounded splendidly and you could hear the balls singing." (Courtesy of Fort Davis National Historic Site.)

Victorio was finally forced back into Mexico and eventually killed by the Mexican army. Of this conflict, Grierson wrote, "by the disposition made of my small force, and the genuine pluck and earnest activity of the troops, Victorio and his bold marauders were three times headed off, twice whipped and driven from their stronghold, and twice forced back into Mexico." The Buffalo Soldiers of the 10th Cavalry proved themselves in battle. This illustration is *Marching on the Mountain* by Frederic Remington. (Author's collection.)

Of the Victorio campaign, historian Robert Leckie wrote, "the real victors were the Buffalo Soldiers of the Ninth and Tenth Cavalry. They had pursued and fought the great chief for thousands of blood spattered miles in an unrelenting contest of courage, skill, endurance and attrition." An African American cavalryman is depicted here in *A Pull at the Canteen* by Frederic Remington. (Author's collection.)

The regimental song of the 10th Cavalry was titled "The Buffalo Soldiers." The lyrics were meant to be sung to the tune of "Camptown Races."

We're fighting bulls of the Buffaloes, Get A'Goin', Get A'Goin',
From the Kansas Plains we'll meet our foes, a trottin' down the line.
Our range spreads west to Santa Fe, Get A'Goin', Get A'Goin',
From Dakota down to the Mexican Way, a trottin' down the line.
Goin' to drill all day, Goin' to march all night,
We've got our money on the Buffalos, somebody bet on the fight!

(Courtesy of Fort Davis National Historic Site.)

One of the men who played a key role in the Victorio campaign was Henry Ossian Flipper, the first African American graduate of West Point. Graduating in June 1877, he was 50th in a class of 75 and was commissioned as a second lieutenant in the 10th Cavalry. During the pursuit of Victorio, Flipper and a small escort made a 22-hour, 98-mile ride to warn Grierson that the Apaches had once again crossed the Rio Grande. Upon the return to Fort Davis, Flipper was appointed quartermaster and commissary officer responsible for feeding and housing the garrison. In this capacity, he handled large sums of government funds. Shortly after Col. William Shafter, 1st Infantry, took command of the post, Flipper came under suspicion of embezzlement. Charged with embezzling $3,791.77 and conduct unbecoming an officer, Flipper went before an Army court-martial made up of white officers. (Courtesy of Fort Davis National Historic Site.)

William Shafter commanded black troops in the Civil War. After the war, he took command of the 24th Infantry. He was considered a superior fighter of Indians and was known as "Pecos Bill" for his exploits in West Texas and southern New Mexico. However, Shafter was also a martinet who played favorites and harassed those he did not like. Subsequent actions would illustrate that he had racist leanings, and as a field officer, he had little interest in the day-to-day administrative duties required to operate a post. Shafter would go on to command American forces in Cuba during the Spanish-American War. When Flipper was arrested, normal procedure dictated that he would be held under house arrest, but initially, Shafter had him confined to the guardhouse. Well liked in the civilian community, several merchants offered to make up the shortfall in Flipper's post accounts. (Courtesy of Fort Davis National Historic Site.)

On November 1, 1881, Flipper's court-martial convened in the post chapel, the ruins of which are shown here. Found innocent of embezzlement but guilty of conduct unbecoming an officer, Flipper was dismissed from service on June 30, 1882. (Photograph by author.)

Flipper moved to El Paso and worked as a mining engineer and surveyor for over 30 years. He worked tirelessly to have his conviction overthrown. In 1976, through the efforts of his family, his discharge was changed to honorable, and in 1999, Pres. Clinton granted him a full pardon. (Courtesy of Fort Davis National Historic Site.)

The death of Victorio and the coming of the railroads (the Southern Pacific and the Texas and Pacific) brought peace to West Texas. For three years, Colonel Grierson and his wife, Alice, presided over Fort Davis. During that time, Grierson oversaw the last surge of construction. He also speculated in land and bought ranch land with the intent of settling in the area after retirement. (Both, courtesy of Fort Davis National Historic Site.)

With a pleasant environment, a new water system, increased quarters for enlisted men and officers, Fort Davis took on the air of a prosperous community. (Both, courtesy of Fort Davis National Historic Site.)

By the late 1880s, the West Texas frontier was mostly settled. By 1885, the Buffalo Soldiers left for duty farther west. Garrison life became routine, and the fort, in the words of Gen. David Stanley, had outlived its usefulness. In 1883, the Southern Pacific Railroad completed a transcontinental line that passed 20 miles south of Fort Davis, and the year prior, the Texas and Pacific, building from the East, connected with the Southern Pacific at Sierra Blanca, passing north of Fort Davis. (Courtesy of Fort Davis National Historic Site.)

With the Indian threat gone, more leisurely pursuits could take place. Here, Lt. Col. Melville Cochran, commanding officer in 1889 and 1890, can be seen returning from a hunt (above), and a group of unidentified men and their ladies (below) are out for a ride. (Both, courtesy of Fort Davis National Historic Site.)

The commanding officer's quarters, as the focal point of garrison life, was always a favorite place for photographs. (Both, courtesy of Fort Davis National Historic Site.)

Taken in the late 1880s, a series of photographs provide priceless documentation of Army personnel at Fort Davis, as well as the style, equipment, and uniforms of the period. Both images are of officers stationed at Fort Davis. (Both, courtesy of Fort Davis National Historic Site.)

These are the noncommissioned officers. The man seated to the far right in the photograph below is Medal of Honor winner Sgt. Thomas H. Forsyth. (Both, courtesy of Fort Davis National Historic Site.)

Grouped informally on this mountainside is Company C of the 3rd Cavalry, which was stationed at Fort Davis between 1885 and 1887 and 1890 and 1891. (Courtesy of Fort Davis National Historic Site.)

A company of the 16th Infantry, stationed at Fort Davis in 1881, from 1882 to 1885, and from 1886 to 1888, is pictured. (Courtesy of Fort Davis National Historic Site.)

A military installation the size of Fort Davis does not exist in a vacuum. From the time the Army arrived on Limpia Creek in 1854 until the fort was abandoned in 1891, civilians were present, supplying the post with everything from beef and hay to vegetables and dairy products. A substantial community developed to the east and south of the post but soon had to find other means of support. (Courtesy of Fort Davis National Historic Site.)

In June 1891, Fort Davis was abandoned, and the land reverted to its original owner, the family of John James from San Antonio. James, a surveyor and speculator, controlled the 640 acres in 1854 and had leased the land to the Army. (Courtesy of Fort Davis National Historic Site.)

Three

A TOWN GROWS UP
1870–1920

From the days of the first fort and the small community called La Limpia, civilians were necessary to support the post, as illustrated by these men hauling wood to supply the hospital. In turn, the Army supplied much of the civilian payroll. Therefore, it was a potential economic disaster when the soldiers left. For the next several decades, it was a struggle to find a new economic base. (Courtesy of Fort Davis National Historic Site.)

Almost from day one, Fort Davis supported a civilian community. Diedrick Dutchover, photographed with his wife, Cora, was here from the beginning. Born Anton Diedrick in 1811 in Antwerp, Belgium, he was shanghaied there and eventually found himself in the hands of Army recruiters in Galveston at the time of the Mexican-American War. Not understanding his name, the recruiter signed him up as Diedrick Dutchallover in the Texas Mounted Volunteers (1848). Soon after, he dropped the "all" from his name. Dutchover and Edward Webster were left in charge of Federal property in 1861. He and Webster were here in the postwar days and saw the town grow. Today, there are many descendants of both in the community. (Courtesy of Fort Davis National Historic Site.)

In the 1880s, the town population was near 800, but then it began a steady decline. The John James family, who owned the post property, attempted to rent out the officer's quarters, but the fort fell into disrepair. Charles Mulhern, a soldier who stayed and became a prominent businessman, wrote, "plenty of houses in Davis now and no one to live in them. The bottom is out of Ft. Davis." (Courtesy of Fort Davis National Historic Site.)

As early as 1850, Presidio County was designated by the Texas Legislature, but it was never organized. Civilian government finally came to Fort Davis in March 1875 when the town became the county seat of Presidio County. An adobe courthouse was constructed on land donated by merchant Whitaker Keesey. A basement jail was excavated beneath the sheriff's office. (Courtesy of Fort Davis Historical Society.)

The Southern Pacific Railroad, the second transcontinental route, bypassed the mountains and passed though Marfa, 20 miles south. Completed in 1883, the line created a crisis over the Presidio County seat. In an election on July, 14, 1885, the voters decided (391 to 302) to move the seat of county government to Marfa. Jeff Davis County was organized in 1887, but a modern courthouse was not completed until 1911. (Courtesy of Mildred Nored.)

The design contract for the new courthouse and a jail was awarded to the architectural firm of L.L. Thurman and Company of Dallas. Design costs were not to exceed $6,000. The construction contract for $47,000 was awarded to the Falls City Construction Company of Louisville, Kentucky. This courthouse remains the centerpiece of Fort Davis and Jeff Davis County. (Courtesy of Fort Davis Historical Society.)

A new jail was constructed to the south of the courthouse. No longer used as a jail, it is one of the county's historical buildings. (Courtesy of Mildred Nored.)

As small as it is, Fort Davis was traditionally divided into three separate communities—Newtown, the section east of the military post; Chihuahua, the section south of Newtown and generally east of the current state highway; and Fort Davis, which developed south of the Army post along the old Overland Trail to the courthouse. In this view from 1912, one can see Newtown across the remains of the old fort. (Courtesy of Fort Davis National Historic Site.)

A small section of the community known as Chihuahua can be seen at the far right in this c. 1910 image. (Author's collection.)

This c. 1910 view of the traditional part of Fort Davis is looking east from the far end of Court Street. A home built by Harry Grierson is visible to the left. (Courtesy of Fort Davis National Historic Site.)

Birds-Eye View, Fort Davis, Texas

This view, taken from the same vantage point as the previous image, dates from several years later, around 1920. (Author's collection.)

Looking from the northwest to the southeast toward Delores Mountain, this image dates from around 1920. Each of the three sections of the community had separate and sometimes duplicated street names. This was not reconciled until 1997. (Author's collection.)

In the first two decades after the Army left, the old Overland Trail, prominently seen here in the 1890s, continued to be the main street of Fort Davis. Most of the town's businesses were clustered along Front and Fort Streets north of the courthouse. (Author's collection.)

In this image is Front Street in Fort Davis, the main thoroughfare in town at the time. One of the town's few stone structures was built in 1906 and purchased by E.H. Carlton in 1911 to be used as a drugstore. In 1928, the Masonic Lodge bought the building and added a second floor. (Courtesy of Martin Stringer.)

STREET SCENE FT. DAVIS, TEXAS

The main street (Front Street) of Fort Davis is seen in this c. 1915 image looking south to north from the intersection of Court Street. (Courtesy of Peter Koch Collection, Archives of the Big Bend, Bryan Wildenthal Library, Sul Ross State University.)

Street and Stewart Hotel Fort Davis Texas

In 1883, William Lempert built a complex of structures one block west of the Overland Trail. He sold this to James Stewart, and it became the Stewart Hotel, which it remained until 1927. Today, it is the Veranda, a bed-and-breakfast. (Courtesy of Fort Davis Historical Society.)

In 1884, while still under the proprietorship of William Lempert, Quanah Parker stayed at the hotel. Parker, a chief of the Comanche and son of the captive Cynthia Ann Parker, established himself as an entrepreneur. This view of the hotel includes the tennis courts across the street. (Courtesy of Fort Davis Historical Society.)

Whitaker Keesey arrived with the Army in 1867 and became the town's premier merchant. His brother Otis arrived in 1870 and opened a general mercantile and saloon in 1873 on the far west side of Chihuahua. Whitaker Keesey patented this section and donated the southwest parcel for the original Presidio County Courthouse. This combination of a store and a courthouse begins the transition of the business center of town to its present location. (Courtesy of Fort Davis Historical Society.)

Otis eventually divorced and moved to California, and W. Keesey and Company became the largest general mercantile establishment in the region. In 1906, the present rock structure was built around the original adobe store. Once complete, the interior adobe building was demolished and removed by wheelbarrow. In this manner, the inventory was protected and the store remained open during the entire process. (Courtesy of Martin Stringer.)

In 1908, a consortium of local businessmen bought out Keesey and created the Union Trading Company. Managed by Walter S. Miller, the Union Trading Company became the hub of the community, and the partnership began to expand its enterprises. This and the following image date from around 1912. (Author's collection.)

Seen here is the interior of the Union Trading Company as it looked after completion and well into the 20th century. (Courtesy of Fort Davis Historical Society.)

In 1911, Keesey began construction of a home. However, his wife became ill, and construction ceased until after her death. The home was completed in 1913, and he died five years later, in 1918. The home was burned in the Rock House fire in April 2011. (Courtesy of Fort Davis Historical Society.)

The expansion of the operations of the Union Trading Company completed the focus of the town center from the old Overland Trail to a different center that was anchored by a new bank and hotel located east of the courthouse. In 1912 and just to the northwest, the company began construction on a new hotel, the Limpia. (Courtesy of Fort Davis Historical Society.)

The Limpia Hotel boasted 12 rooms, an expansive lobby, a dining room, kitchen, and a carbide gas plant for lighting. (Courtesy of Fort Davis Historical Society.)

Fort Davis State Bank was organized in 1911, the same year Whitaker Keesey donated land southwest of the mercantile to the Independent Order of Odd Fellows (IOOF). In 1913, the IOOF and the bank joined forces to construct a two-story building, with the bank on the ground floor and the IOOF lodge above. (Courtesy of Fort Davis Historical Society.)

On March 31, 1913, ground was broken for the Fort Davis State Bank. Many of the shareholders were also partners in the Union Trading Company. (Courtesy of Fort Davis Historical Society.)

By 1915, the town square boasted the Union Mercantile, the Limpia Hotel, and Fort Davis State Bank. The new Jeff Davis County Courthouse is in the background. (Courtesy of Fort Davis National Historic Site.)

In the late 19th century and well into the 20th century, fraternal organizations were an important part of the social fabric. Besides the IOOF, there was also an active Union Veterans organization, the Grand Army of the Republic, and a Masonic lodge in Fort Davis. In 1928, the Masons bought the former Carlton building and added a second floor. (Courtesy of Fort Davis Historical Society.)

The community of Fort Davis always had a strong Catholic presence, and the first parish was organized in 1876. Daniel Murphy donated land for a church in 1905, and a building was constructed soon after. The present St. Joseph's, to the right, was constructed in 1896 and is still in use. The building on the left is the original church, and the rectory is in between. (Courtesy of Fort Davis Historical Society.)

The Methodists organized the first Protestant church in 1884 on land donated by Whitaker Keesey. This was the first Protestant building between San Antonio and El Paso. Modernized and expanded, it is still in use today. (Courtesy of Fort Davis Historical Society.)

A Presbyterian congregation first met in March 1884 in a private home. With the arrival of Rev. William B. Bloys, a church was organized in March 1884 and a building constructed in 1904 on the slope of Sleeping Lion Mountain, the highest Protestant church in Texas. In 1928, with the building in place, a basement was excavated under the sanctuary for use as a fellowship hall. (Courtesy of Vivian Grubb.)

The Baptist congregation was organized in a private home in 1896 and initially met in the Methodist church. They purchased a commercial building in 1921 and constructed their present building in 1942, completing the fourth historic church. (Courtesy of Fort Davis Historical Society.)

Isolated as they were, many of the ranch families created their own schools or sent their children away. In Fort Davis, schools were segregated, and there were private academies. The first two dedicated school buildings were the South School, seen below, near the courthouse (1887) and the North School (around 1880) shown above, where classes were held on the ground floor and the IOOF met upstairs. (Both, courtesy of Fort Davis Historical Society.)

In 1902, an election was held to provide funding for a new, modern school built just to the south of the Presbyterian church. The new but segregated school opened in 1904. It is seen here with the Presbyterian church to the right. In keeping with segregation, a Hispanic school was also constructed in Chihuahua. (Courtesy of Martin Stringer.)

Dating from after 1911, this view shows the new school, the Presbyterian church, and the new Jeff Davis County Courthouse; the old school building is in the distance. (Courtesy of Fort Davis National Historic Site.)

A1028 Bird Orchard, the largest Apple Archard in Texas Near Ft. Davis Tex.

The mountainous terrain discouraged major farming around Fort Davis, but in the first decades of the 20th century, Fort Davis was known for apples. There were several orchards, the largest of which was planted by C.H. Bird in 1908 and 1909. It consisted of 60 acres and had 3,300 trees. Today, the Teague family continues the tradition with an orchard along Limpia Creek, just north of town. (Author's collection.)

Apples were packed for transport and kept in sheds such as these. Due to the climate, Fort Davis apples ripened earlier and were often some of the first to market. (Courtesy of Mildred Nored.)

The high virgin grasslands of the Davis Mountains were perfect for raising cattle. Raising beef to supply the garrison brought some of the first settlers to the region, and ranching remains an economic mainstay today. Upon retirement from the Army, Benjamin Grierson went into ranching and land speculation. These photographs are of the Grierson ranch headquarters. (Above, courtesy of Fort Davis National Historic Site; below, courtesy of Illinois State Historical Library, Springfield.)

The first cattle in the region were longhorns, but they were soon replaced by shorthorns, especially Herefords, which proved especially well adapted to the range environment of the Davis Mountains. Jim and Beau McCutcheon are said to be among the first to import Herefords. Their ranch was in the north part of the county. (Courtesy of Martin Stringer.)

In 1919, a group of regional ranchers organized the Highland Hereford Breeders Association to improve and promote the breed and "for the purpose of fostering the sale of cattle grown in this area and to assist in and encourage the growing of better cattle." The Highland Hereford persisted as the breed of choice well into the 20th century. Pictured is a branding scene on the U-up U-down Ranch. (Courtesy of Martin Stringer.)

While a number of men from Fort Davis marched off to World War I, the concern over the border troubles with Mexico were closer to home. The Mexican Revolution began in 1910, and internal conflict in that country continued into the 1920s. The Army had a major presence on the border with a garrison at Camp Marfa, 20 miles to the south. Training marches were common, with troops bivouacking on the abandoned Fort Davis parade ground, as photographed here in 1922. (Both, courtesy of Fort Davis National Historic Site.)

The old fort continued to be a focal point for the community. The officer's quarters were used as residences and the grounds for a variety of activities, including a Fourth of July celebration (above) on the porch of the hospital and a Cinco de Mayo celebration (below), both pictured in the mid-1890s. The parade ground was often used as a baseball field. (Both, courtesy of Fort Davis National Historic Site.)

Like most communities, Fort Davis has had its share of characters. Nick Mersfelder (1858–1939), born in Germany and a barber by trade, joined the Texas Rangers Frontier Battalion in 1881. Settling in Fort Davis, he had a barbershop and served as justice of the peace. A good musician who played several instruments, Mersfelder also was a photographer. He owned the first automobile in the county, as well as a bicycle. (Courtesy of Fort Davis National Historic Site.)

Mersfelder owned a building, part of which was his home and the other part was an office for his various enterprises. Today, this structure is maintained by the Fort Davis Historical Society and operated as the Overland Trail Museum. (Courtesy of Fort Davis National Historic Site.)

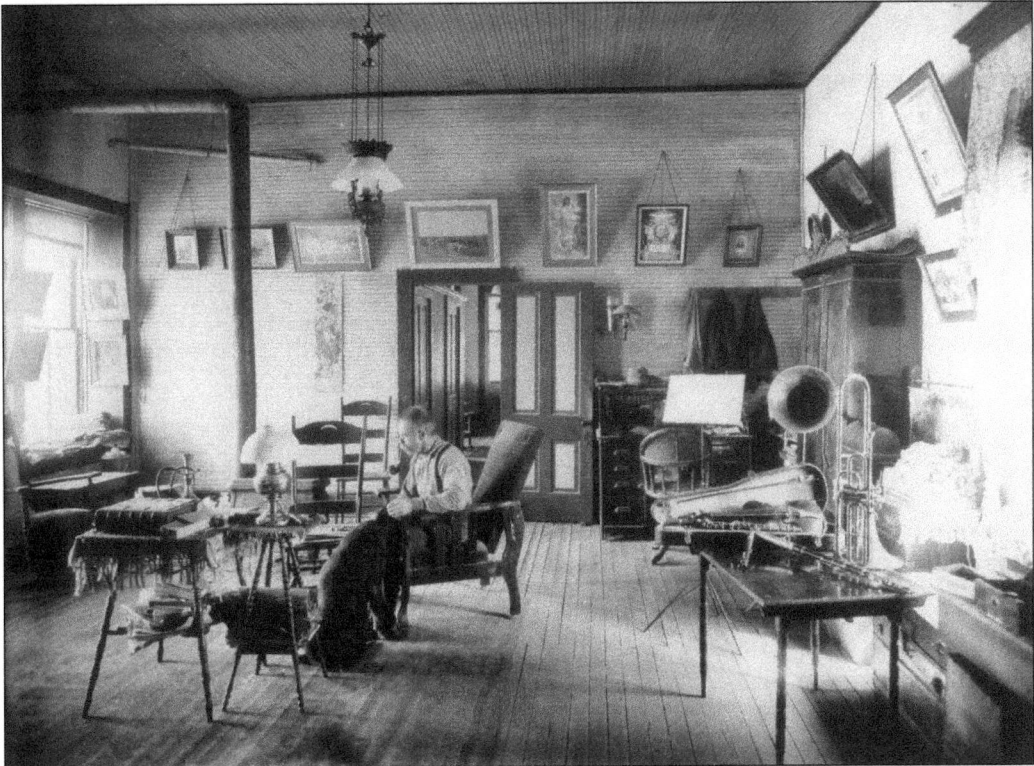

Until after World War I when the automobile began to overtake railroads as the primary method of transportation, tourism represented a minor part of the town's economy. However, the mountainous climate had a great appeal to many people, which they could enjoy if they were able to make the trip on primitive roads, such as the one between Fort Davis and Alpine. (Courtesy of Martin Stringer.)

It was intrepid travelers, such as the men seen here in 1909, who braved the primitive Davis Mountains with poor roads and few visitor services or facilities. (Author's collection.)

Four

SURVIVING THE DEPRESSION AND WAR
1920–1960

After the Army left, ranching became the mainstay of the area, and the ranching tradition remains an important and integral part of the economy. However, from the 1920s through World War II and beyond, other factors began to impact development. Tourism and astronomy found their place in the economy of Fort Davis. When the McDonald Observatory was completed in 1938, its 82-inch mirror made it the second largest telescope in the world. (Author's collection.)

For the ranchers in the Davis Mountains and the Big Bend region, the beef animal of choice continued to be the Highland Hereford, as seen here. (Author's collection.)

The Story of the Highlands

In 1936, the Highland Hereford Breeders Association published *The Story of the Highlands* to advertise and promote the breed. (Author's collection.)

Roundups and branding were held each spring, and the cattle were shipped in the fall. (Author's collection.)

The chuckwagon, such as this one on the o6 Ranch, was an important part of the roundup. (Author's collection.)

Noonday on the X Ranch

The cook seems to have numerous satisfied customers after a morning's work on the X Ranch. (Courtesy of Martin Stringer.)

It was the cowboy who made ranch operations work. These two men are working a Merrill Ranch roundup. (Courtesy of W.D. Smithers Collection, Fort Davis Historical Society.)

Before air-conditioning, the cool, dry mountain summers began to attract visitors to Fort Davis. W.S Miller, proprietor of the Limpia Hotel, came up with the term "summer swallows" to describe the visitors. Finding a place to stay for the season became difficult, and several families built homes. The home built by the Wallis and Knox families of Houston is used as the Baptist parsonage today. (Courtesy of Fort Davis Historical Society.)

Henry M. Truehart of Galveston built his home at the end of Court Street. Today, it is a guesthouse operated by the Limpia Hotel. (Courtesy of Fort Davis Historical Society.)

The ruins of the old Army post fascinated visitors even as it slowly deteriorated, as seen in these photographs from the 1920s. (Both, courtesy of Fort Davis National Historic Site.)

For the first half of the 20th century, the old fort remained in the hands of the John James estate, and little was done to protect this valuable resource. (Both, courtesy of Fort Davis National Historic Site.)

In 1929, Jack Hoxie—star of over 1,000 western B movies, including *Thunderbolt Jack* and *Ridin' Thunder*—acquired the rights to use the fort and billed it as the Hoxie Stockade and Motion Picture Studio. A victim of the Great Depression, by 1931, the effort had failed. Here, Hoxie and Dixie Starr (second and third from the left), his leading lady, are seen with members of the Higgins family. (Courtesy of Fort Davis National Historic Site.)

To generate interest in the enterprise that was to include a golf course, tennis courts, a pavilion, a dude ranch, and his movie studio, Hoxie hosted a rodeo and Wild West show on March 23, 1930. Over 3,000 people made their way to Fort Davis for the event. (Courtesy of Fort Davis National Historic Site.)

A serious effort to promote tourism began with the Texas Legislature in 1927 when state senator Thomas Bell of Dallas introduced a bill instructing the Highway Department to develop the Davis Mountains State Park Highway through the heart of the mountains. The project began with an initial appropriation of $10,000. It was not until January 1932 that grading crews began their work, starting north and west along Limpia Creek. (Courtesy of Fort Davis Historical Society.)

THROUGH THE DAVIS MOUNTAINS
ON THE
DAVIS MOUNTAINS STATE PARK HIGHWAY

SIXTY SCENES OF TEXAS' MOST BEAUTIFUL SUMMER PLAYGROUND, SHOWING STATE PARK IN KEESEY CANYON; McDONALD OBSERVATORY, NOW UNDER CONSTRUCTION ON MOUNT LOCKE; BLOYS CAMPMEETING GROUNDS, CATTLE PICTURES AND SCENES ALONG THIS ROUTE, COMMONLY KNOWN AS "THE SCENIC DRIVE."

To promote the construction of the Davis Mountains State Park Highway, which was intended to be one of the first linear scenic highway parks in the country, the Fort Davis Chamber of Commerce engaged noted West Texas photographer W.D. Smithers to document the project. Coincidentally, his work occurred at the same time as construction of the McDonald Observatory and the development of Davis Mountains State Park by the Civilian Conservation Corps. (Courtesy of W.D. Smithers Collection, Fort Davis Historical Society.)

In 1926, William J. McDonald of Paris, Texas, bequeathed $1.1 million to the University of Texas for an observatory. Relatives contested the will, and the bequest was eventually reduced to $800,000. At the time, the University of Texas did not have a department of astronomy, so the school partnered with the University of Chicago, which had astronomers but not a major telescope. The first instrument was an 82-inch reflecting telescope. (Author's collection.)

Otto Struve, director of Chicago's Yerkes Observatory, was selected to head the project. The first order of business was site selection. When Struve arrived in Fort Davis, he met W.S. Miller, who was always ready to promote his community. Here, Dr. Struve (left) and Dr. Christian Elvey are seen at one of their camps on a site-selection visit. The astronomers agreed on a location to the northwest of Fort Davis. (Courtesy of Fort Davis Historical Society.)

The land in question belonged to the U-up U-down Ranch, which was founded in the 1880s by Dr. George Scott Locke from New Hampshire. By 1933, his granddaughter, Violet Locke McIvor, was managing the ranch and donated 200 acres to the Davis Mountains State Park Highway. The ranch headquarters remain in the family. (Courtesy of Julie and Scott McIvor.)

W.S. Miller was instrumental in persuading Violet Locke McIvor, pictured here with her grandfather G.S. Locke, to donate 200 acres to the university (in addition to the land already donated to the Davis Mountains State Park Highway project). The location for the observatory was named Mount Locke, and an adjoining 200 acres donated by the estate of Edwin Fowlkes was named Mount Fowlkes. Construction could finally begin. (Courtesy of Julie and Scott McIvor.)

A road, the continuation of the Davis Mountains State Park Highway project, was built in 1933 to provide access to the top of Mount Locke. A construction contract was let to the Warner and Swasey Company of Cleveland, Ohio, for the observatory dome, mirror, and telescope housing. The most critical part of the work was the pouring of the mirror by the Corning Glass Works in Pennsylvania and the subsequent delicate polishing that created the 82-inch, 4,000-pound optical instrument. (Courtesy of W.D. Smithers Collection, Fort Davis Historical Society.)

On November 10, 1933, ground was broken on Mount Locke. After the foundation was constructed, the steel dome, which was fabricated in Cleveland, was hauled to the top of the mountain and erected. Workers lived in tents, and transportation from the railroad in Marfa (more than 30 miles away) was over roads yet unpaved. (Courtesy of W.D. Smithers Collection, Fort Davis Historical Society.)

The first two levels of the observatory dome were designed as offices, quarters, a lecture hall, and a library, while the third level housed the 90,000-pound telescope, its mount, and associated instruments. The 60-foot diameter dome had to rotate 360 degrees. The telescope itself was mounted on two concrete piers anchored in bedrock and rotated on two axes, allowing it to be pointed at any portion of the sky. (Courtesy of W.D. Smithers Collection, Fort Davis Historical Society.)

The official dedication ceremony was held May 5, 1939, with preeminent scientists and astronomers from throughout the world in attendance. In addition to the observatory, several residences and support structures were built. Here, the completed dome can be seen behind the director's home. (Courtesy of W.D. Smithers Collection, Fort Davis Historical Society.)

Construction on the roadway towards McDonald Observatory was well underway when Companies 879 and 881 of the Civilian Conservation Corps arrived in June 1933 to set up camp in Keesey Canyon, five miles northeast of Fort Davis. The Civilian Conservation Corps was a Great Depression federal recovery program that employed young men and provided them training, jobs, and family income while working to conserve public lands and create parks. (Courtesy of Martin Stringer.)

The Davis Mountains State Park Highway was uniquely designed to be a linear park or scenic driving parkway, not a park in the traditional sense. In the midst of the Great Depression, the State Parks Board and the Civilian Conservation Corps created the conventional Davis Mountains State Park. Nestled in Keesey Canyon the park possesses one of the most exceptional hotels in the state, Indian Lodge. (Courtesy of W.D. Smithers Collection, Fort Davis Historical Society.)

Civilian Conservation Corps Company 881 departed in November 1933, but Company 879 labored on until July 1935, working on campgrounds, support buildings, and the Indian Lodge. Architect Bill Caldwell created the design for the lodge from typical southwestern adobe designs. The original furnishings were built by the Civilian Conservation Corps at Bastrop State Park, not locally. The 16-room hotel in its unique mountain setting became famous throughout Texas. (Author's collection.)

Part of the development of the Davis Mountains State Park was a five-mile scenic road that, through a series of switchbacks, climbed to the top of North Ridge—the mountain that creates the part of the canyon that protected the old Army post. At the end, they constructed a stone overlook that provided a spectacular view of the old fort. Skyline Drive is still a favorite of visitors today. (Courtesy of W.D. Smithers Collection, Fort Davis Historical Society.)

The idea of a linear park receded as the Davis Mountains State Park and Skyline Drive took precedence in the public's mind, but the concept remained important. In the centennial year of 1936, the legislature instructed the Highway Department to give it priority, stating that "it is highly important that the thousands of Centennial visitors from other states shall have the opportunity of visiting and inspecting this Great Texas Mountain Area." (Courtesy of W.D. Smithers Collection, Fort Davis Historical Society.)

The Davis Mountains State Park Highway, now known as Scenic Loop, is 75 miles of natural beauty through the heart of the mountains. It was not actually completed until after World War II. It was dedicated on June 28, 1947, twenty-one years after the initial effort began. The ribbon was cut by Anton Aggerman, the last surviving soldier to have served at Fort Davis. (Courtesy of Fort Davis Historical Society.)

When Pearl Harbor was attacked, Fort Davis supplied its share of service personnel. Numerous men and women from the county served. Although the military was long gone from the community, the Army still maintained an area presence through Fort D.A. Russell in Marfa. Troops were often seen on maneuvers in the rugged terrain around Fort Davis. They were also in the occasional parade down main street, including this one in 1938. (Both, courtesy of Fort Davis National Historic Site.)

The most decorated soldier from the community was Sgt. Manual Gonzales, who distinguished himself at Salerno, Italy, by destroying four German machine guns and a mortar. Later, at Monte Casino, he destroyed a German tank. Wounded in both engagements, he was awarded a Silver Star and the Distinguished Service Cross, which was presented by Gen. Mark Clark on Christmas Day in 1943. A statue of this hero graces the Jeff Davis County Courthouse lawn. (Photograph by author.)

The Great Depression drove cattle prices down, and they did not recover until the war years. From 1900 to 1950, the town grew slowly in population from 1,150 to 2,090. What tourism was possible during the Depression years and the development of McDonald Observatory did help the economy, but the character of the town changed little. (Author's collection.)

Major changes occurred in the Fort Davis schools. In May 1929, bonds in the amount of $60,000 were issued for a new segregated central school that was completed and opened in February 1930. Today, this building houses the junior and senior high school classes. (Courtesy of Fort Davis Historical Society.)

In 1939, additional bonds in the amount of $30,000 were issued for a new Hispanic school at the north end of town on the state highway. Opened in September 1940, it was named for Mattie Anderson, a Fort Davis teacher in the 1880s and 1890s. Today, it serves as the elementary school for Fort Davis. (Courtesy of Fort Davis Historical Society.)

The advances in radio wave communication in World War II created an interesting connection to Fort Davis. Funded by the US Air Force, the Harvard Radio Astronomy Station began operations in August 1957 with the purpose of studying solar flares that disrupted communications. The Fort Davis location was perfect because of the isolation and lack of residual radio interference. The solar program at the station ended in 1982. (Courtesy of Dr. Alan Maxwell.)

Located on Cook Flat at the Sproul Ranch, the 28-foot dish tracked the sun from sunrise to sunset. In conjunction with facilities in Germany and Australia, it helped maintain a 24-hour-a-day watch on the sun, greatly increasing scientific knowledge. The director of the station from 1957 to 1983 was Dr. Alan Maxwell, a Harvard faculty member. He is pictured here (right) with colleagues Sam Goldstein (left) and Govind Swarup. (Courtesy of Dr. Alan Maxwell.)

Five

CAMP MEETINGS, DUDES, AND CELEBRATIONS
1890–PRESENT

Tradition has always been strong in the community, as has the proprietary feeling about the old fort. This view is of Fort Davis in 1961, at the time it became part of the National Park System. The love of a ranching heritage and old Army tradition, the unique mountain scenery, the unspoiled environment and the pleasant climate help to bring recurring visitors. Dude ranches, camp meetings, and celebrations provide education and entertainment for all. (Courtesy of Fort Davis National Historic Site.)

William Benjamin Bloys (pictured here with his wife, Mabel) started his Presbyterian ministry in Coleman, Texas. In 1888, he moved to Fort Davis for health reasons. He would often travel between widely spread ranches. In 1889, John Z. and Exa Means suggested organizing a camp meeting. The next year, on October, 10, 1890, forty-seven people attended the first meeting, thus, the Bloys Campmeeting was born. It has continued for 120 years. (Courtesy of Bloys Campmeeting Centennial Exhibit.)

The second year, a brush arbor was erected to accommodate the attendees. From the beginning, Bloys declared, "every denomination is welcome here. There will be no line drawn because of different religious beliefs." The Bloys Campmeeting Association was officially organized in 1904. With $1,250 in donations, it purchased a section of land, Skillman Grove, where the association still meets. The brush arbor sufficed until it was replaced by a tent in 1902. (Courtesy of Bloys Campmeeting Centennial Exhibit.)

The camp meeting became so successful and important to the families in the region that a permanent frame and metal tabernacle were constructed in 1912. However, most families continued to erect tents and cook from their ranch chuckwagons. The new tabernacle, which has been expanded several times, is to the left in this c. 1915 image. It is surrounded by numerous tents. (Courtesy of Bloys Campmeeting Centennial Exhibit.)

As the camp meeting grew, chuckwagons were no longer sufficient. Soon, the attendees organized themselves into family groups, or camps, and constructed cookshacks. Today, there are six such camps, and most members have constructed permanent cabins that may only be used during the week of the camp meeting. Finances are handled by donation to the various camps and to the association. (Courtesy of Bloys Campmeeting Centennial Exhibit.)

By the 1930s, the camp meeting became like a town unto itself for a week each year in August as the families gathered. The Presbyterian minister in Fort Davis, following in the footsteps of William Bloys, is superintendent, and each year a Baptist, Methodist, and Disciples of Christ minister is asked to speak. When Smithers took this photograph (around 1935), the camp meeting was a significant part of the life and culture of Fort Davis. (Courtesy of W.D. Smithers Collection, Fort Davis Historical Society.)

The Prude family arrived in the 1880s, and for much of the 20th century and into the present day, their name has been associated with dude ranching, summer camps for boys and girls, and tourism. To supplement their ranching income, the family began to take in guests, or "dudes," in the 1920s. John G. Prude and his wife, Ruth, took over in 1940 and started a summer camp for boys in 1951. (Courtesy of Betty Prude.)

Involved in the boys' camp from the beginning, John Robert Prude and his wife, Betty, moved to Fort Davis in 1959. Summer camp expanded to include girls, and the facility grew to accommodate over 400 campers during each two-week session. The draw for Prude Ranch Summer Camp was always the horses. Every camper had his own, and the session finished with a rodeo. The corral was always a popular place. (Courtesy of Betty Prude.)

Prude Ranch has always been a family operation. By now, second- and third-generation campers are returning, and numerous couples have met and married at the Prude Ranch. Three generations of Prude men are pictured here in the horse corrals (from left to right): Andy, John G. "Big Spurs," Charles, John Robert, and Chipper. Countless visitors have enjoyed the hospitality of the Prude family. (Courtesy of Betty Prude.)

PRUDE RANCH, FORT DAVIS, TEXAS

In a typical scene from the late 1950s, boys from the summer camp are off to town for a soda pop at the Fort Davis Drug Store; John G. Prude is in the lead. (Author's collection.)

Old Fort Davis Army Post

Centennial

FORT DAVIS, TEXAS

October 9-10, 1954

CELEBRATION ORGANIZED AND CONDUCTED BY
FORT DAVIS HISTORICAL SOCIETY

The issue of preservation of the old fort continued to plague many members of the community. On February 18, 1953, in the home of concessionaires Malcolm "Bish" and Sally Tweedy on Officers' Row, the Fort Davis Historical Society was created for the "acquisition and preservation of the old Fort Davis Army Post." The first order of business was to organize a centennial celebration to draw attention to the cause. (Author's collection.)

The centennial celebration began with a parade that started at the hospital. John G. Prude, president of the society, led the parade, followed by a uniformed color guard. The celebration included a pageant, a band concert, a barbecue served by the Odessa Chuck Wagon Gang, a rodeo, and dances. (Courtesy of Fort Davis Historical Society.)

Upon organization, the historical society leased the fort and took over the operation of the trading post and museum, a block building constructed on the foundation of one of the old barracks. They also established a horse rental concession, which was operated by the Prude Ranch. The purpose was to maintain the fort and promote its preservation by the state or federal government. Here, the centennial parade begins at the hospital ruins. (Courtesy of Fort Davis Historical Society.)

It seemed as if everyone in town participated in the celebration. Keesey Miller, who owned Nick Mersfelder's old runabout, and his wife, Lillian, dressed for the occasion and put the old car in running order. Numerous other families brought out their old buggies and wagons for the festivities. (Courtesy of Fort Davis Historical Society.)

The celebration and the efforts of the historical society were successful. On January 3, 1961, Rep. J.T Rutherford of Odessa introduced a bill in Congress to make the fort a National Historic Site. The bill passed and was signed by Pres. John F. Kennedy on September 8, 1961, purchasing 447 acres. Rutherford (at the far right) attended the centennial and is pictured here with, from left to right, H.L. Winfield, John Prude, Roxa Medley, and Barry Scobee. (Courtesy of Fort Davis Historical Society.)

National Park Service personnel arrived in January 1962 and immediately began operations to restore one of the barracks for offices, a visitors' center, and a museum. They also started a massive stabilization effort that included replacing roofs and porches on many of the historical structures. However, it was not until April 4, 1966, that the official dedication took place. (Courtesy of Fort Davis National Historic Site.)

The fort dedication was the culmination of the efforts of the entire community. From this point on, Fort Davis National Historic Site would be a permanent and important part of the community. Annually, thousands would visit to learn about Army life on the frontier and the story of the Buffalo Soldiers. Over 7,000 people were in attendance at the dedication. (Courtesy of Fort Davis National Historic Site.)

Dedication Ceremonies
Fort Davis National Historic Site
April 4, 1966

10:00 a.m. Concert .... High School Bands
10:30 a.m. Band Honors to Mrs. Lyndon B. Johnson
    Marfa High School Band - Conducted by Travis Branaman
    Alpine High School Band - Conducted by Wayne Maxwell
    Marathon High School Band - Conducted by James Bates
    Pecos High School Band - Conducted by Bill Carrico
    Invocation .... Rev. Hugh Stiles
        First Baptist Church, Fort Davis
    Introduction of Distinguished Guests .... Hon. Gene Hendryx
        Representing the Sponsoring Organizations
    Welcome to Fort Davis .... Supt. Franklin G. Smith
    Introduction of Hon. Richard C. White
        Hon. George B. Hartzog, Jr., Director, National Park Service
    Remarks .... Hon. Richard C. White
        Congressman, 16th District, Texas
    Remarks and Introduction of Hon. Stewart L. Udall
        Hon. George B. Hartzog, Jr.
    Introduction of Mrs. Lyndon B. Johnson
        Hon. Stewart L. Udall, Secretary of the Interior
    Dedication Address .... Mrs. Lyndon B. Johnson
    Formal Raising of the Thirty-Seven Star Flag
        Period Music by 62nd and 424th Army Bands
        United States Army Air Defense Center
            Fort Bliss, Texas
        C.W.O. Herbert Bilhartz, Conductor
    Artillery Color Guard of the United States Army Artillery
        and Missile Center, Fort Sill, Oklahoma
    Benediction .... Father Anthony Bertasius
        St. Joseph's Catholic Church, Fort Davis
11:30 a.m. Public Barbecue, Odessa Chuck Wagon Gang
1:00 p.m. Public Band Concerts .... High School Bands
3.30 p.m.
    &   Retreat Parade Sound Program
4:30 p.m.

The keynote speaker for the dedication was Claudia Alta "Lady Bird" Johnson, wife of Pres. Lyndon Johnson and First Lady of the United States. She is accompanied by Secretary of Interior Stewart Udall. Franklin G. Smith (seen in park service uniform to the left and behind Udall) was the second superintendent of Fort Davis and instrumental in establishing many of the interpretive programs visitors enjoy today. (Courtesy of Fort Davis National Historic Site.)

After the First Lady's speech, a new 37-star flag was raised. There was food and period music. However, preservation efforts did not cease. Eventually, the commanding officer's quarters were furnished, followed by restoration of a junior officer's quarters, an enlisted barracks, the commissary, and a kitchen. (Courtesy of Fort Davis National Historic Site.)

Sesquicentennial Celebration
Events Schedule
October 9, 2004

Time	Activity	Location
8:00 am	Fort Opens	
9:00 am	Sesquicentennial Grand Parade	Along the Historic San Antonio – El Paso Road (Fort Street)
10:30 am	Morning Gun & Flag Raising	Parade Ground
10:45 am	Sesquicentennial Ceremony	Large Tent
11:30 - 1:00 pm	Barbecue	Large Tent
11:45 am	Alpine Community Band Concert	Large Tent
1:00 - 2:30 pm	Auction	Large Tent
1:00 – 4:00 pm	Children's Games & Activities	Commanding Officer's Quarters
1:00 pm	Nicodemus Buffalo Soldiers Program	Buffalo Soldiers' Camp
1:30 pm	Stamp Cancellation Ceremony	Officer's Quarters #4
2:00 pm	Infantry Drill & Small Arms Demonstration	Parade Ground
2:30 pm	Cavalry Drill & Small Arms Demonstration	Parade Ground
3:00 pm	The Sweet Song String Band Concert	Large Tent
3:30 pm	Artillery Drill & Demonstration	Parade Ground
4:00 pm	Cavalry Drill & Presentation	Parade Ground
4:30 pm	Sidesaddle Demonstration	Parade Ground
5:00 pm	Drawing for Raffle Items Beard Judging	Friends Booth
5:15 pm	Flag Lowering & Evening Gun	Parade Ground
5:30 pm	Fort Closes	
7:00 pm	Historic Ball	Prude Ranch

SESQUICENTENNIAL CEREMONY
10:45 A.M.

Invocation..Reverend Joe Gossett

Welcome & Introduction of Special Guests......Todd W. Brindle
Superintendent
Fort Davis NHS

Recognition of Fort Descendants..................Mary Williams
Historian
Fort Davis NHS

Guest Speakers.....................................Brigadier General
Charles B. Allen
4th Infantry Division
(Mechanized)
ADCS

G. Martin Merrill
Past President
Fort Davis Historical Society

Robert M. Utley
Chief Historian (Retired)
National Park Service

National Historic Landmark Dedication
Closing Remarks......................................Todd W. Brindle
Superintendent

Benediction...Reverend Joe Gossett

In 1983, the Friends of Fort Davis was organized to support the preservation and living history efforts of the Park Service. Each October, the organization sponsored a festival for this purpose. Not to be outdone by prior celebrations, the Friends of Fort Davis and the park staff hosted a sesquicentennial celebration in October 2004. Men of the 4th Infantry Division, direct descendents of the 8th Infantry, were honored guests and speakers. (Author's collection.)

The sesquicentennial celebration began with a parade starting at the high school and proceeding down the old Overland Trail. Once again, the Odessa Chuck Wagon Gang served barbecue, as they had at the centennial and dedication. A large tent, 200 living history interpreters, and a historical evening ball at the Prude Ranch were some of the many activities held during the day. (Courtesy of Max Kandler.)

Over 200 reenactors, men and women from throughout the state, took part in the celebration. The day at the fort began by raising the garrison flag and firing the morning gun (a three-inch ordnance rifle) and ended with lowering the flag and firing the evening gun. (Courtesy of Max Kandler.)

Among the reenactors was Company F of the Nicodemus, Kansas, Buffalo Soldier Association. Some members of the association are direct descendants of the original Buffalo Soldiers. Their camp was a favorite place for visitors. (Courtesy of Max Kandler.)

Six

A Destination Attraction
1960–Present

"On this the 13th day of June, A.D. 1927, came on to be heard the application of a number of county officials of Jeff Davis County for an order of the Commissioners' Court prohibiting loafers from loitering in the Court House yard or on the Court House fences." The courthouse, restored in 2003, is today the centerpiece of the community. (Courtesy of Max Kandler.)

As the age of space exploration dawned, there was a need for larger and better astronomical instruments. In 1968, with funding from NASA, the University of Texas dedicated a new 107-inch telescope, now named after former observatory director Harlan J. Smith. At the time it was built, the telescope was the third largest in the world and used in the exploration of the solar system. (Courtesy of McDonald Observatory.)

The mirrors of most telescopes are one piece of glass, which restricts their maximum size. In 1997, the University of Texas and a consortium of other schools dedicated the Hobby-Eberly Telescope (HET) Observatory. The 36-foot-diameter mirror is made up of 91 hexagonal segments. Currently, the telescope is involved in the Hobby-Eberly Telescope Dark Energy experiment designed to unlock one of the major secrets of the universe. (Courtesy of McDonald Observatory.)

In 1969, when the first astronauts landed on the moon, one item left behind was a small reflector. Using a powerful laser and the 107-inch telescope, scientists at McDonald Observatory were able to determine that the moon was actually 40 meters farther away than expected and . moving about 1.5 inches farther each year. These laser-ranging studies, using a variety of instruments throughout the world, now help study continental drift. (Courtesy of McDonald Observatory.)

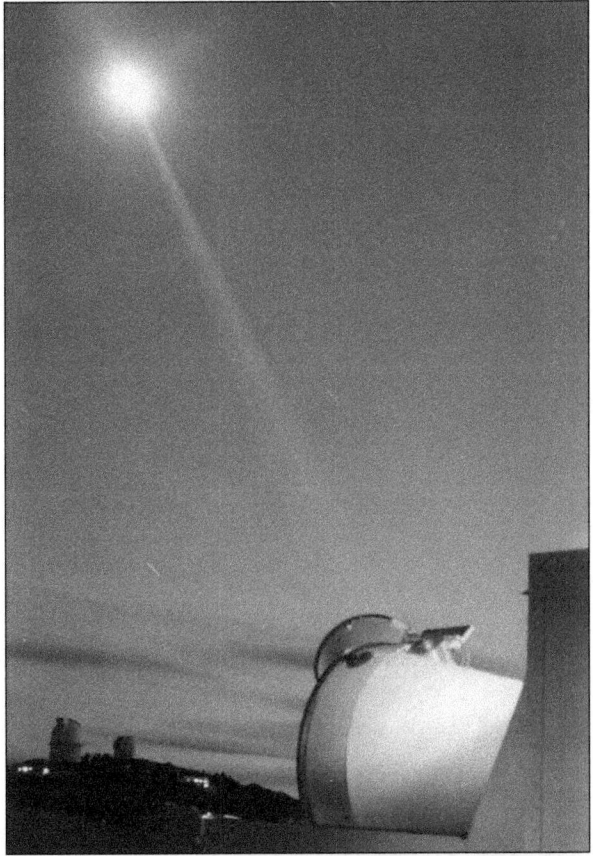

The original William McDonald bequest to the University of Texas included a stipulation that part of the mission promote astronomy. To accommodate the thousands of visitors from around the world, the University of Texas constructed the Frank Bash Visitors Center that includes an amphitheater, a theater, exhibits, a gift shop, and the StarDate Café. "Star parties" were held several nights week. (Courtesy of McDonald Observatory.)

In 1962, the Harvard Radio Telescope facility expanded with the construction of an 85-foot-diameter antenna and new laboratory. Besides tracking the sun, this instrument was used to study pulsars, quasars, and other radio wave objects. The station ceased operations in 1991. Now a component of the National Radio Astronomy Observatory, it is part of the Very Long Baseline Array that links facilities from several locations into one. (Photograph by author.)

In 1996, the Prude Ranch was recognized by the Texas Historical Commission for its part in the heritage of the region and its role in the development of tourism. The facility operates year-round for groups and families, and the summer camp continues to attract children from far and wide. (Courtesy of Betty Prude.)

Because the State of Texas had done little upkeep for Davis Mountains State Park, in 1959, J.W. Espy sued for the return of the 169 acres he had originally donated. When Espy won his case, he returned the land on the condition that the state protect this asset. In late 1965, work began that created a new Skyline Drive and improved the campgrounds. (Courtesy of Chase Fountain, Texas Parks and Wildlife.)

As part of the improvements to the park, Indian Lodge was expanded to 39 rooms, including a modern restaurant and a swimming pool. Booked most of the year, the Indian Lodge is recognized as one of the truly unique places to stay in Texas. (Courtesy of Chase Fountain, Texas Parks and Wildlife.)

Fort Davis National Historic Site continues to have a thriving living history program. The Friends of Fort Davis, under the direction of former and now retired superintendent Jerry Yarbrough, began a program to restore the post hospital—architecturally, it is an important 19th-century public building. Active in the living history program, Yarbrough stands to the left of the muzzle, ready to load the cannon. (Courtesy of Max Kandler.)

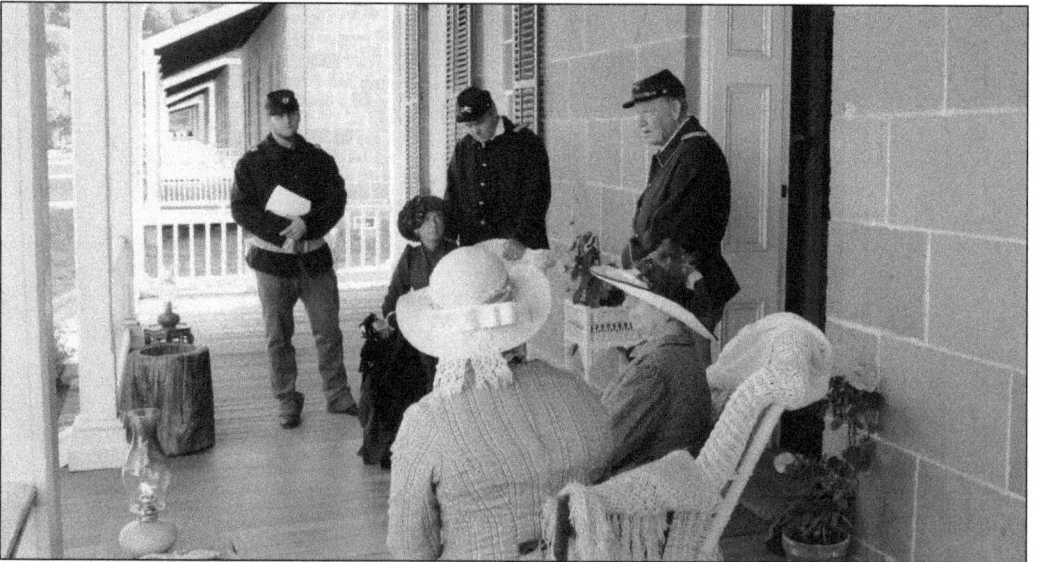

Living history and interpretive activities include an 1870s retreat parade and several buildings furnished in the period style. During spring break or major holidays, the cannon crew is often busy on the parade ground with the three-inch ordnance rifle. Each October, the park staff and the Friends of Fort Davis host a late-afternoon barbecue and lantern-light tour based on historic events of the period. (Courtesy of Max Kandler.)

The Chihuahuan Desert Research Institute was founded in 1974 as a research organization dedicated to gathering and disseminating information about the region. The headquarters, the Chihuahuan Desert Nature Center, is located on over 500 acres of grasslands and canyon lands on the road to Alpine. The facility includes an arboretum, greenhouse, visitors' center, exhibits, and information on native plants. (Courtesy of Chihuahuan Desert Research Institute.)

The Chihuahuan Desert Nature Center offers the visitor over five miles of hiking trails, one of which heads down into Modesta Canyon. The canyon features natural springs and numerous native plants and birds. Another trail leads to an overlook with an exhibit on area geology that interweaves the history and culture of the mountains into the geologic narrative. (Courtesy of Chihuahuan Desert Research Institute.)

For many years, the Union Trading Company building was vacant. Acquired by Jeff Davis County and restored with funds from the Texas Department of Transportation, the structure reopened in 1999 and now houses the public library and offices of the Fort Davis Chamber of Commerce and the community's official visitors' center. (Courtesy of Max Kandler.)

The Limpia Hotel is the centerpiece of commercial historic preservation. Reaching beyond the town square, the owners, Joe and Lanna Duncan, have acquired three of the oldest historic homes in Fort Davis (the Truehart House, the Mulhern House, and the Dr. Jones House), operating them now as guesthouses. In addition, they have restored the Stone Village Motor Court and the Stone Village Grocery, turning it into a modern delicatessen. (Courtesy of Limpia Hotel.)

In 1926, Hunter and Annie Lou Clark purchased the Stewart Hotel and converted it into apartments. Hunter died in 1953, and Annie Lou managed the apartments for several more decades, supplementing her income by teaching music to most of the children in the community. Now operated as the Veranda Bed & Breakfast, it was recognized in 1910 as the best bed-and-breakfast in the West by *True West* magazine. (Courtesy of David Schrieber.)

Records indicate that when the old school, located south of the Presbyterian church, was replaced in 1930, it was sold to F.M. Miller for $15,000. Over time, the structure has undergone various renovations, including the removal of parts of the original. It has been used as an apartment complex and as a single-family dwelling. It is now operated by Carla and Steve Kennedy as the Old Schoolhouse Bed & Breakfast. (Courtesy of Steve and Carla Kennedy.)

The H.S Sproul ranch was established in 1886 by Robert S. Sproul. It is one of the oldest ranching operations in the county, and in the mid-1950s, when Harvard University was seeking a location for its radio telescope, the Sproul family generously agreed to a 25-year lease at no fee. Utilizing the former site, Tony and Kerith Sproul Timmons manage the Harvard Lodge, which includes the Harvard Hotel in town. (Courtesy of Rhonda Hole.)

Davis Mountains Lodge and Expeditions, located at the old Spencer Motor Court on the Alpine highway, has operated an Elderhostel program for more than a decade. Elderhostel is a nonprofit organization (now called Road Scholar) that is based in Boston. It offers educational travel programs. In addition, Davis Mountains Lodge and Expeditions offers facilities, educational programs, and cabin rentals to groups and families. (Courtesy of Davis Mountains Lodge and Expeditions.)

In 1998, the Texas Nature Conservancy purchased the Upper Ranch of the U-up U-down Ranch from owner Don McIvor. That acquisition, plus others, created the 36,000-acre Davis Mountains Preserve. The preserve encompasses Mount Livermore, the second highest peak in Texas, and many of the old ranch buildings. The new McIvor Education Center is the Nature Conservancy Headquarters for the preserve. (Courtesy of Texas Nature Conservancy.)

When the Scenic Loop road was dedicated in June 1947, the ceremony was held at the Lawrence Wood picnic area in Madera Canyon. Still a favorite spot for a picnic, in 2007, the Texas Nature Conservancy opened a 2.5-mile hiking trail that loops through the Davis Mountains Preserve. Since the preserve is only open on special occasions, this allows visitors the luxury of experiencing the beauty of the mountains. (Courtesy of Texas Nature Conservancy.)

Every July, the Fort Davis Chamber of Commerce sponsors the Coolest Fourth of July in Texas. The high, dry climate usually guarantees the visitor a lower temperature than anywhere else in the state. A parade through town, barbecue on the courthouse lawn, frontier bank robberies, vendors, a dance, living history events at the fort, and fireworks make this an old-fashioned Fourth of July that should be experienced by all. (Courtesy of Chuck Nowland.)

Over the years, the community has received a number of awards, but none as prestigious as the one received in 2008 when the National Trust for Historic Preservation listed Fort Davis as one of its Dozen Distinctive Destinations. State representative Pete P. Gallego was on hand to congratulate the community. (Courtesy of Max Kandler.)

FURTHER READING

For the in-depth history of the numerous pioneer families that have lived in Fort Davis for decades, please see *Fort Davis* by Lucy Jacobson and Mildred Bloys Nored, published by the Fort Davis Historical Society. The society also operates the Overland Trail Museum, the former home of Nick Mersfelder, on Front Street.

The visitor to Fort Davis who may be interested in seeking out many of the old homes and businesses will find *Early Homes and Buildings of Fort Davis* by Mildred Bloys Nored and Jane Wiant helpful. These volumes are available at the Limpia Hotel gift shop. The Fort Davis Chamber of Commerce in the Union Building also has a map of many of the historic buildings; it can be used either as a walking or driving tour map.

The Fort Davis National Historic Site Visitors Center has a book selection that is excellent. For the person seeking information on Indians, the Army in the West, the Buffalo Soldiers, frontier Army life, and published diaries and journals, the visitors' center is the place to go.

For a history of the fort itself, the National Park Service handbook by Robert Utley is an excellent short history. A more in-depth study can be found in *Frontier Crossroads: Fort Davis and the West* by Robert Wooster. The history of the Buffalo Soldiers is told in Robert Leckie's book by that title, and frontier Army life is written about in *Forty Miles a Day on Bend and Hay* by Don Rickey. *Unlikely Warriors* by Robert and Shirley Leckie is the story of the lives of Benjamin Henry Grierson and Alice Kirk Grierson.

Big and Bright by David Evans and J. Derrel Mulholland provides the history of the McDonald Observatory, and the Frank Bash Visitors Center has numerous books on the history and science of astronomy.

POSTSCRIPT

As a postscript to this story of Fort Davis, on April 9, 2011, one of the largest wildfires in Texas history roared through the town and county. The Rock House fire began in Marfa, over 20 miles away, and within two hours was in town, destroying over 20 homes. Local, state, and federal resources fought the fire for three weeks before it was contained. Firefighters and equipment came from all over the country to help. Eventually burning 315,000 acres, almost 500 square miles, this fire was devastating to Jeff Davis County. Luckily, there were no fatalities and, in fact, no major injuries. However, many ranchers lost all or most of their grazing land and over 300 miles of fence, a catastrophe of major proportions to those who make a living in the cattle business.

The fire crossed over onto the Fort Davis National Historic Site and the Davis Mountains State Park, where efforts on the part of firefighters were able to protect these valuable resources before any structures were burned. The fire also threatened McDonald Observatory and the Chihuahuan Desert Research Institute, and two historic structures in town were destroyed, the Keesey Mansion (pictured in this book) and the Carlton Home.

Wildfire is a fact of life in these desert mountains but devastating nonetheless. Luckily, the community is resilient, and there is a culture of neighbor helping neighbor. To steal a line from William Faulkner, "we shall not only endure, we shall prevail."

Visit us at
arcadiapublishing.com

www.ingramcontent.com/pod-product-compliance
Lightning Source LLC
Chambersburg PA
CBHW050621110426
42813CB00007B/1679